THE LITTLE BOOK OF COCKTAIL TIPS

CR

THE LITTLE BOOK OF COCKTAIL TIPS

CRAIG EDNEY

A.
Absolute Press

First published in Great Britain in 2010 by
Absolute Press, an imprint of Bloomsbury Publishing Plc
Scarborough House, 29 James Street West
Bath BA1 2BT, England
Phone 44 (0) 1225 316013 **Fax** 44 (0) 1225 445836
E-mail office@absolutepress.co.uk
Web www.absolutepress.co.uk

Reprinted 2014.

A catalogue record of this book is available from the British Library
ISBN 13: 9781904573975
Printed and bound by Hung Hing, China

Bloomsbury Publishing Plc
50 Bedford Square, London WC1B 3DP | www.bloomsbury.com
Bloomsbury is a trademark of Bloomsbury Publishing Plc.

‘I feel sorry for people who don’t drink.
When they wake up in the morning,
that’s as good as they’re going to feel
all day.’

Frank Sinatra

1

Avoid making a drink stronger than the recipe

– it's better to have two perfect cocktails than one overpowering one. Drinking should be about enjoyment, not getting drunk.

2

To make **the perfect cosmopolitan,**

combine 35ml vodka (preferably Citron vodka), 20ml Triple sec or Cointreau, 3 drops of orange bitters, 20ml cranberry juice and 20ml fresh lime juice with ice in a cocktail shaker. Serve straight up in a martini glass garnished with a piece of orange zest.

3

Most cocktails are made up of

three essential ingredients:

something sweet, something sour and a spirit. A great example is the Caipiroska, made up of whole limes, brown sugar and Cachaca, all muddled together.

4

Why not **make a jug of cocktails for** when your **guests** arrive? Just follow a recipe and increase to the amount of guests coming.

A great start to the evening would be a long juice cocktail like a Summer Breeze: 140ml each of vodka, cloudy apple juice and cranberry juice and 50ml of elderflower cordial, served in a long glass over ice with a cape gooseberry on top.

5

When muddling a Mojito always twist your wrist

instead of plunging in and out of the glass; the idea is to mulch all the limes, sugar and mint together.

6

One of the reasons **brown sugar** is added to a Mojito is **to grate** the flesh and skin of **the lime and extract** as much lime **juice and zest** as possible.

7

When making cocktails, if you are using **heavy ingredients** they **need to** be **shaken vigorously** in order to be mixed. To mix cocktails using this technique use either a Boston or a three piece, fill the shaker/glass with ice and add the ingredients in order of alcohol content. Place the lid on holding one hand over the top and one hand on the base and shake vertically, making sure the drink travels the full length of the shaker.

8

Most shaken drinks which contain light cream can also be made as blended drinks,

substituting vanilla ice cream for the light cream.

9

So how long do you shake for?

Some drinks require more than others but a good way to tell is when the water starts condensing on the outside of the shaker, this indicates that the cocktail is chilled enough. Once shaken, strain into your desired glass and enjoy the fruits of your labour!

10

Blending cocktails with an electronic blender is a great technique to use

when you are **faced with ingredients that will not mix well** together or those that can't be shaken or stirred.

11

When making frozen cocktails less is definitely **more when** it comes to **adding crushed ice.** Be sure to add it last and a little at a time until you get the right consistency, otherwise you might end up with nothing more than a slushy mess.

12

Layering

may prove a little tricky at first!

Start with the heaviest spirit

or highest sugar content and add this to the glass. Then add the next spirit by pouring it over the back of a teaspoon, touching the edge of the glass and the top of the previous spirit so the liquid is poured over the teaspoon to form a layer.

13

To determine which spirits are heavier or lighter than others think of it this way;

the lower the alcohol content

the more sugar there is, therefore,

the denser the spirit is. Remember,

the sweetest and lowest proof spirit should always be poured in first.

14

The Essentials: to set up your bar you will need...

bottle opener; corkscrew; can opener; measuring cups and spoon set; bar spoon with long handle and muddler on the end; juice squeezer; electric blender; cutting board and a sharp knife; ice bucket with an ice tong; mixing glass; shaker and strainer; boxes or jars to store garnishes in; glassware; cocktail napkins and coasters; swizzle sticks; straws (both long and short ones); sugar and salt (for coating the rims of glasses)... and perhaps this book!

15

The golden shaking rules:

use 6 to 9 ice cubes; hold the shaker horizontally with both hands in front of your shoulders and shake vigorously back and forth; shake for about 10 to 20 seconds; shake as hard as you can: shake it awake, don't rock it to sleep!

16

To make sugar syrup,

use equal parts of castor sugar and water and heat in a saucepan until the sugar has dissolved. Allow to cool.

17

Avoid pre-squeezed lemon or lime juice, or concentrates, as they lack that fresh burst of flavour that comes from a fresh lemon or lime. This probably is the most important hint of all:

avoid all bar mixes and artificial concentrated substitutes.

18

Quality not quantity.

Always try to use high-quality spirits that have been distilled a number of times. A rough guide is

the more distillation the better the spirit,

but shop around and you will find good products for reasonable prices.

19

Measure everything!

The importance of measuring cocktail ingredients cannot be stressed enough if you want to

create great tasting drinks consistently.

Many people skip this step because it's time-consuming, however, measuring ensures that you are creating the cocktail in the correct way every time.

20

The cornerstone of cocktail-making is the

understanding of **the relationship between strong and weak, sour and sweet.**

'Strong' refers to the main alcoholic component of the drink, such as vodka, rum or gin. 'Weak' means the lesser alcoholic beverages such as liqueurs. 'Sour' means mainly citrus fruits such as lemon or lime. 'Sweet' accounts for sugar and syrups.

21

Tools of the trade: the majority of the professional tools mixologists use can either be found quite easily online or **can be substituted** for everyday household items, such as a jigger egg cup for a measure, a thermos flask for a cocktail shaker, a small rolling pin or the end of a wooden spoon for a muddler.

22

To make the perfect Mojito,

place two lime quarters in a glass. Add 5ml of Gomme syrup (or 2 cubes of brown sugar) with 50ml of gold rum and muddle together, making sure you squeeze the juice out of the limes. Fill with crushed ice and top up with soda (or apple juice for an apple Mojito). Add 6 mint sprigs and tease to the bottom of the glass with a spoon, gently lifting the lime, sugar and rum upwards.

23

To make a classic Martini,

first fill a cocktail glass with ice and leave to one side. Pour 50ml of gin (or vodka) and 15ml of dry vermouth into the glass and fill with ice cubes. Slowly stir until the ice dilutes the drink to your taste. Once the set-aside ice-filled glass is very cold to the touch, discard the ice and strain in the drink, adding your choice of garnish: fruit zest, cherry, caper berry or an olive.

24

For a Margarita,

first fill a glass with ice and leave to one side. Into a cocktail shaker, add 37.5ml of tequila, 25ml of Cointreau or triple sec, 12.5ml of lime juice and fill with ice. Shake vigorously for 45 seconds to a minute. If you intend to salt the rim of the glass, pour either table salt or sea salt onto a small plate, rub the rim of the glass with lime and roll in the salt. Strain the drink into the glass and serve.

25

Try to

avoid milky or creamy drinks at the beginning of the evening.

They tend to sit in your stomach, making you feel bloated. Try drinking crisp, clean cocktails like fruit-based martinis and save the creamy ones for later.

26

Don't – whatever you do – put fizzy drinks in the shaker!

Always add the fizzy stuff afterwards.

27

Don't overwork yourself

at your own party by trying to make six different drinks! My biggest cocktail party tip is to

limit your offerings

to three cocktails with different spirit bases. You wouldn't offer your dinner guests a four page menu, so don't do it for cocktails either.

28

Wine makes you think of silly things,

beer makes you say them, but

cocktails make you do them.

29

Flavoured vodkas:

don't splash out when you can

make them at home.

Remove 50ml of vodka from the bottle and add your chosen fruit. Raspberries work particularly well, so add around 20 raspberries to the vodka, leave for two weeks to infuse, then: hey presto! Raspberry vodka. Watermelon and lychee also work well with vodka.

30

This flavouring technique (see previous tip) works really well with **Pimms and gin** too. Remove 50ml of gin from the bottle, add half a roughly chopped cucumber and leave **for** two weeks to infuse. Next time you're making your Pimms punch, add in 25ml of your cucumber gin to give it **a fresh summery dimension**.

31

For something a bit more autumnal,

why not try mixing blackberry and apple with either gin, vodka or winter Pimms?

32

One popular method of decorating cocktails is

frosting

which leaves an edge of sugar, salt, cocoa, or any other fine powder on

the rim of the glass.

Rub the rim of the glass with a slice of orange or lemon, then submerge the rim in sugar or salt (or any other powder) so that it lines the top of the glass.

33

Ice: one of the most important ingredients needed to make most cocktails. Make sure you **have plenty of it and use it generously.**

Cocktails served at room temperature don't taste as nice as ice-cold ones.

34

If you haven't got a cocktail shaker

why not clean out an old jam jar
with a tight lid and use that instead?

35

A cocktail menu is

an economical way of entertaining

since it means you won't have to stock every spirit under the sun and will, instead, just need the ingredients to cover the few drinks you're offering.

36

Never use crushed ice when shaking

as the ice will melt and dilute the cocktail.

37

When stirring a cocktail **you will need** a glass or metal mixing rod, sometimes referred to as **a 'swizzle stick'.**

It is best to use a mixing glass when stirring and then strain into your desired glass. When water is condensing on the outer side of the glass, the cocktail is ready to drink.

38

Make it look pretty: garnishes help a drink look more appealing and appetizing.

If something looks good, it will probably taste better

but as with all cocktails the right amount is the key; if it takes you a few minutes to dig through the garnishes before you can start drinking, there is something wrong!

39

Match the drink and glass temperature.

When you are serving cold drinks, chilling the glass before pouring will keep the drink colder longer. This can be as simple as placing a glass in the freezer for a minute or pouring cold water or ice into the glass while you are shaking the cocktail, then discarding it before you pour out the drink.

40

To make a Mint Julep

add 4 mint springs, 2 teaspoons of caster sugar and a couple of tablespoons of crushed ice to a glass and 'massage' with a spoon. Breaking or crushing the mint makes the flavour sour, so be sure to gently fold and stir. Add 25ml of rye whisky or rum, more crushed ice and continue massaging. Fill with ice, pour in another 25ml of whisky or rum and add a dash of soda, if desired.

41

If you need to chill wine or Champagne quickly, place the bottle in an bucket of ice and throw in some salt; the salt freezes the ice quickly to below its usual freezing point, making your bottle chill faster.

42

Cocktails can be made prior to the event

in a large bowl, covered and kept in the refrigerator until the party begins. If you're making sangria or Pimms, freeze the fruit the night before and this will act like ice in the drinks.

43

Nothing is worse than having a great drink that everyone is enjoying, and then having to switch them over to wine or beer when it runs out too soon.

For a 3-hour party, plan on two to three drinks per person, but make more than you'll need – you may need to sip one when you're cleaning up that night!

44

Practice making all your drinks ahead of time.

Set all your garnishes out

in glass bowls and your mixers in pitchers. Not only does this help you assemble drinks quickly, but your guests are more likely to ask for a drink if they see all the ingredients set out.

45

General rule of thumb:

for four or less

guests **intricate and blended cocktails are best** served; for larger parties – dust off the fruit bowl.

46

Cocktail books often describe
some liquids served as a dash:

**a dash is
one eighth of
a teaspoon.**

47

Free pouring.

Assuming you are using a tapered pourer on your bottles, 25ml of spirit is equal to 2 'counts'; 35ml equals 3 counts; 50ml equals 4 counts. So, to measure 35ml of spirit,

count '1001... 1002...1003' as you are pouring.

After a while, you should be able to do it by eye.

48

To make highballs, fill a glass two-thirds full of ice before adding liquor.

Always pour liquor in before the mixer.

Do not stir drinks containing carbonated mixers.

49

To make cocktails lowball,

and other shaken or stirred drinks,

fill a shaker half-full of ice before pouring

the drink.

50

The most important thing is to

experiment and have fun.

Try building your own cocktails based on the foundations in this book. Next, try making some of your favorite cocktails, starting with the simpler ones with fewer ingredients and working your way up.

Measurement conversion tables

The majority of cocktail books come from America and they have a different measuring process to the UK. The best rule of thumb is to remember a 25ml UK single measure is near to one American fluid ounce (29.6ml), so when following US recipes slightly pour over the 25ml measure.

1tsp	–	⅓tbsp	5ml
1tbsp	½ fl oz	3tbsp	15ml, 15cc
2tbsp	1fl oz	⅛ cup, 6tsp	30ml, 30cc
¼ cup	2fl oz	4tbsp	59ml
⅓ cup	2⅔ fl oz	5tbsp & 6tsp	79ml
½ cup	4fl oz	8tbsp	118ml
⅔ cup	5⅓ fl oz	10tbsp & 2tsp	158ml
¾ cup	6fl oz	12tbsp	177ml
⅞ cup	7fl oz	14tbsp	207ml
1 cup	8fl oz/½pt	16tbsp	237ml
2 cups	16fl oz/1pt	32tbsp	473ml
4 cups	32fl oz/2pt	1 quart	946ml

Craig Edney

Craig Edney has been at the sharp end of the hospitality industry for more than twenty years, building up an outstanding pedigree at the very top of the industry. He has opened bars and run events all over the world, from New York to Miami, from Sydney to Singapore. Craig founded and manages Hydromel Ltd, one of the UK's leading mobile cocktail bar specialists and has provided award-winning bespoke cocktail bars to a host of stars and celebrities. He works closely with Jamie Oliver to consult and train bar staff at his Italian restaurants as they open across the world. His favourite cocktail is a dry gin martini. Stirred.

www.hydromelevents.com

THE LITTLE BOOK OF
BRIDGE
TIPS
PETER FRENCH

THE LITTLE BOOK OF
CHESS
TIPS
PETER FRENCH

THE LITTLE BOOK OF
FISHING
TIPS
NICK DEVENISH

THE LITTLE BOOK OF
GREEN
TIPS
WILLIAM FORTT

THE LITTLE BOOK OF
KITTEN
TIPS
ANDREW LANGLEY
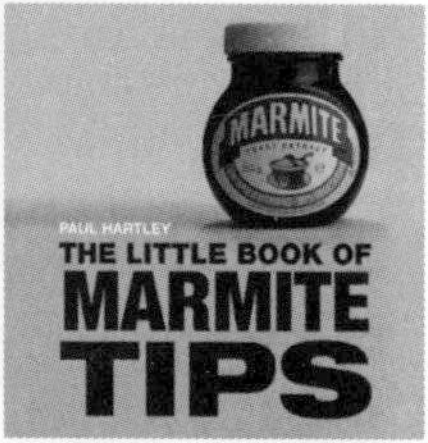
MARMITE
PAUL HARTLEY
THE LITTLE BOOK OF
MARMITE
TIPS

THE LITTLE BOOK OF
PUPPY
TIPS
ANDREW LANGLEY

THE LITTLE BOOK OF
WHISKY
TIPS
ANDREW LANGLEY

THE LITTLE BOOK OF
TRAVEL
TIPS
MEGAN DEVENISH